GRAPHIC SCIENCE

THE ILLUMINATING WORLD OF LIGHT

with MAX AXIOM SUPER SCIENTIST

by Emily Sohn

illustrated by Nick Derington

Consultant:
Leslie Flynn, PhD
Science Education, Chemistry
University of Minnesota

Mankato, Minnesota

Graphic Library is published by Capstone Press,
151 Good Counsel Drive, P.O. Box 669, Mankato, Minnesota 56002.
www.capstonepress.com

1 2 3 4 5 6 12 11 10 09 08 07

Library of Congress Cataloging-in-Publication Data
Sohn, Emily.
The illuminating world of light with Max Axiom, super scientist / by Emily Sohn;
illustrated by Nick Derington.
p. cm.—(Graphic library. Graphic science)
Summary: "In graphic novel format, follows the adventures of Max Axiom as he
explains the science behind light"—Provided by publisher.
Includes bibliographical references and index.
ISBN-13: 978-1-4296-0140-5 (hardcover)   ISBN-10: 1-4296-0140-X (hardcover)
ISBN-13: 978-1-4296-1768-0 (softcover pbk.)   ISBN-10: 1-4296-1768-3 (softcover pbk.)
1. Light—Juvenile literature. 2. Adventure stories—Juvenile literature. I. Derington,
Nick, ill. II. Title. III. Series.
QC360.S645 2008
535—dc22   2007002264

Art Director and Designer
Bob Lentz

Cover Artist
Tod Smith

Editor
Christopher L. Harbo

Photo illustration credits: iStockphoto, 23; Shutterstock/Jo-Hanna Wienert, 13

TABLE of CONTENTS

With a sudden flash of lightning, Super Scientist Max Axiom begins an adventure in light.

CRACK!!!

What was that?

It's okay, Spark. It's just a little thunder and lightning from a passing storm.

WHIMPER...WHIMPERRR...

Actually, Spark, if you could understand how light works, things like lightning wouldn't be so scary.

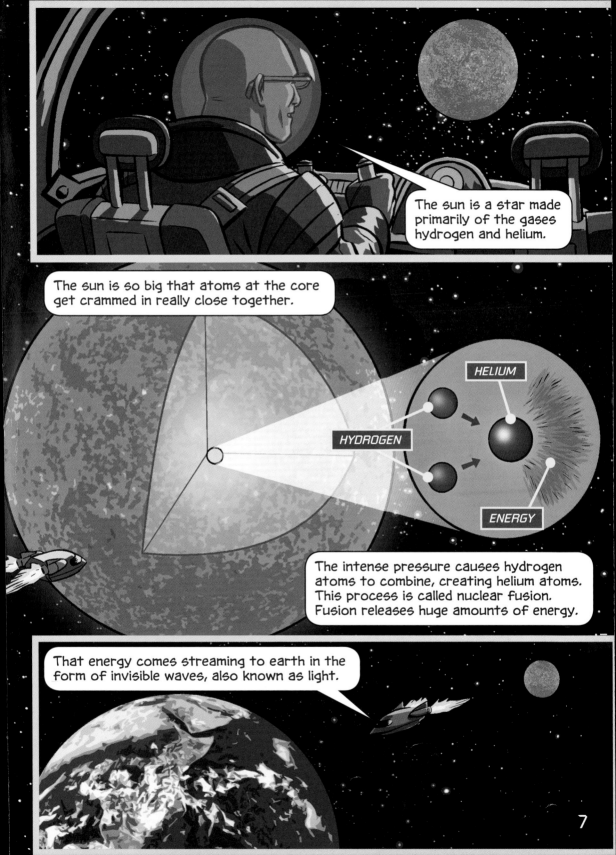

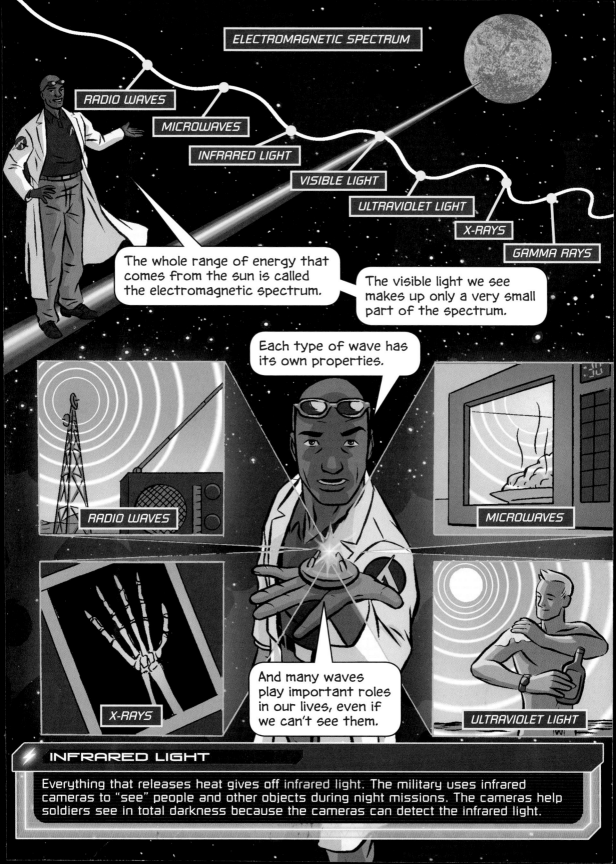

ELECTROMAGNETIC SPECTRUM

RADIO WAVES

MICROWAVES

INFRARED LIGHT

VISIBLE LIGHT

ULTRAVIOLET LIGHT

X-RAYS

GAMMA RAYS

The whole range of energy that comes from the sun is called the electromagnetic spectrum.

The visible light we see makes up only a very small part of the spectrum.

Each type of wave has its own properties.

RADIO WAVES

MICROWAVES

X-RAYS

ULTRAVIOLET LIGHT

And many waves play important roles in our lives, even if we can't see them.

INFRARED LIGHT

Everything that releases heat gives off infrared light. The military uses infrared cameras to "see" people and other objects during night missions. The cameras help soldiers see in total darkness because the cameras can detect the infrared light.

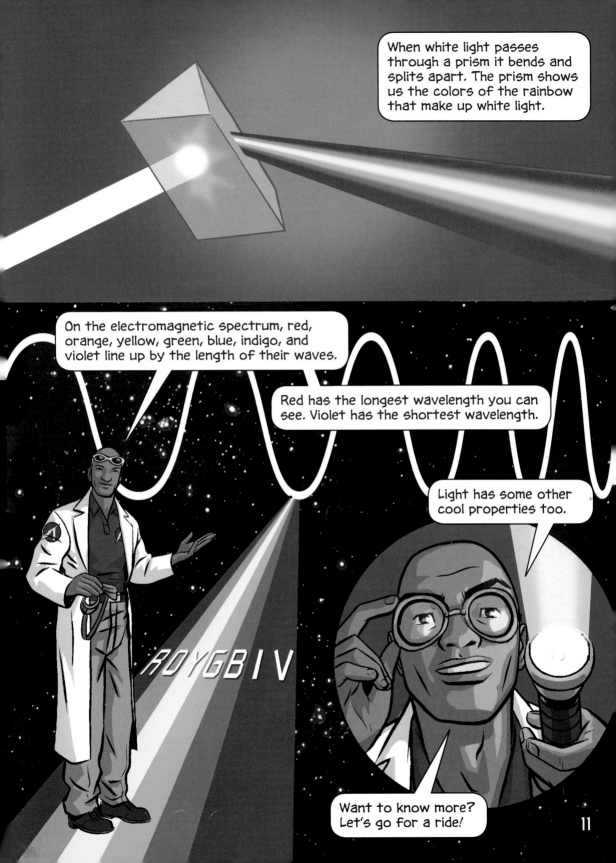

Although light moves superfast, we can see how it behaves when it hits objects around us.

For instance, have you ever wondered why you can see yourself in a mirror?

It's because light bounces off shiny surfaces and back to your eyes.

This bouncing is called reflection.

REFLECTION

Light reflects off more than just mirrors. Everything you see reflects some light. For example, you can see the moon because sunlight reflects off its surface and into your eyes.

One of the most important things we do with light is see.

Let's take a look at how our eyes use light.

The human eye is only about 1 inch tall and 1 inch wide, but it's a complicated organ.

CORNEA

Light comes in through the cornea and travels to the pupil.

PUPIL

The pupil changes size to let in more or less light, depending on how bright it is outside.

1 inch = 2.5 centimeters

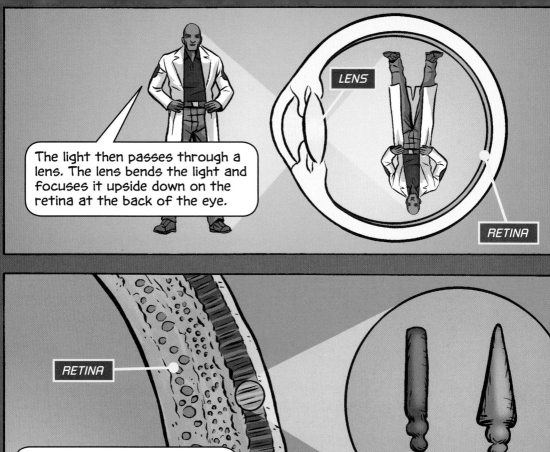

The light then passes through a lens. The lens bends the light and focuses it upside down on the retina at the back of the eye.

LENS

RETINA

RETINA

The retina has two types of cells called rods and cones. Rods sense black and white. Cones sense color and details.

ROD

CONE

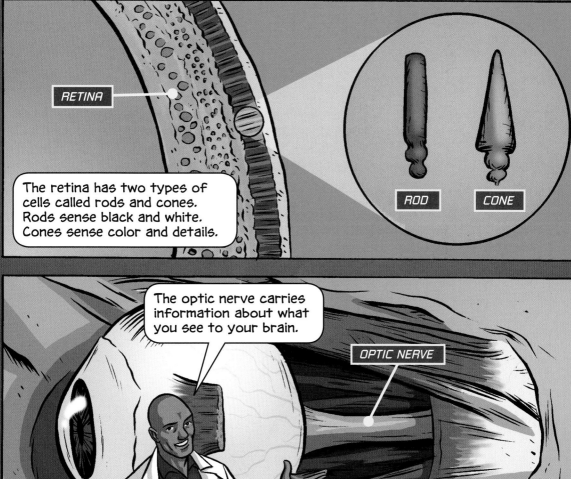

The optic nerve carries information about what you see to your brain.

OPTIC NERVE

Your brain turns the images it receives back over so you see the world right side up.

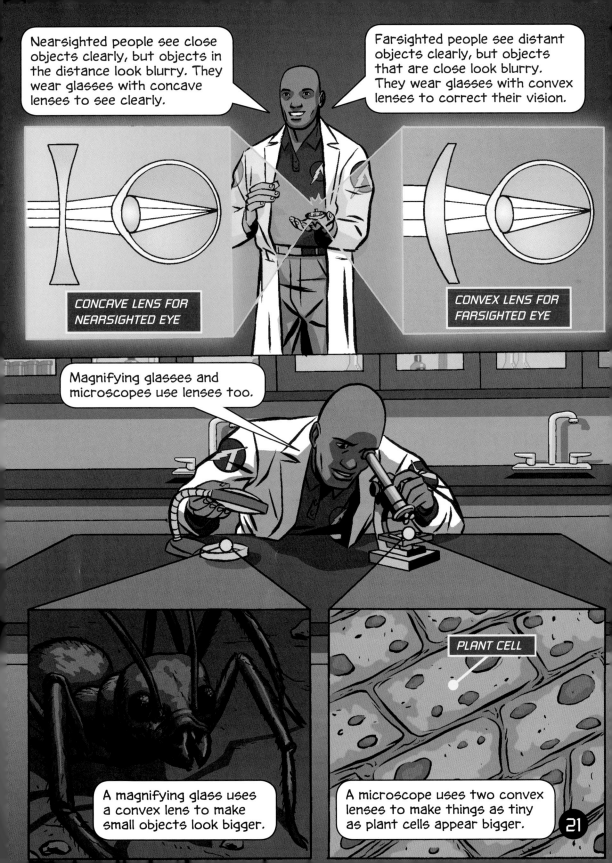

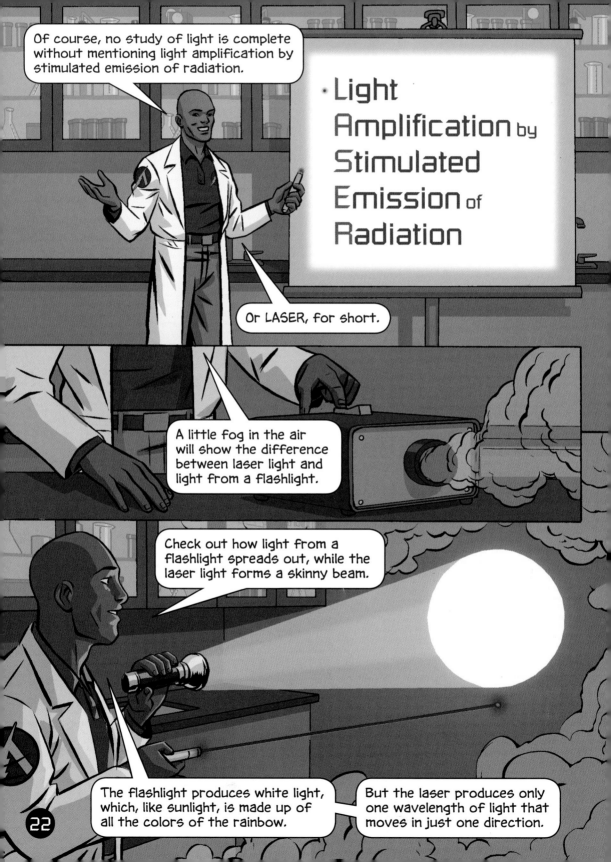

24

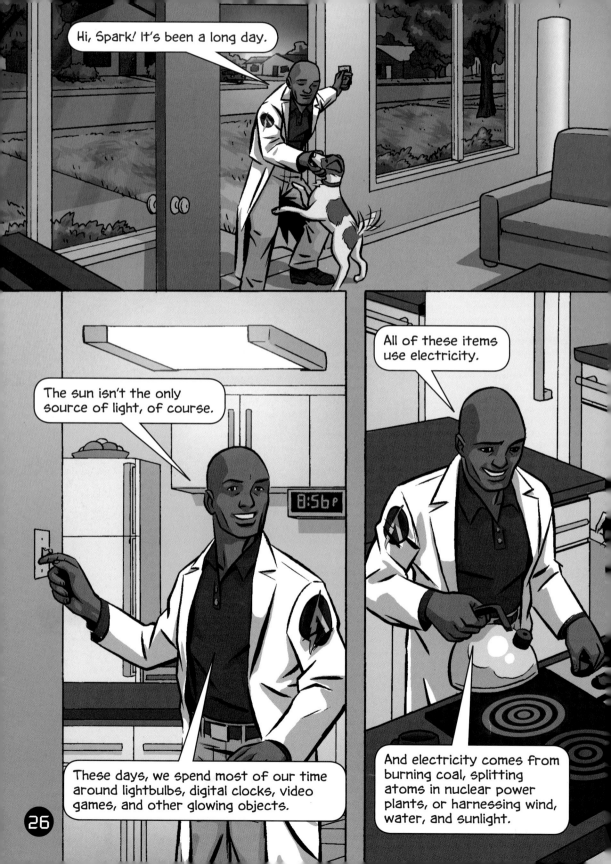

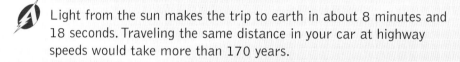

MORE ABOUT LIGHT

Light from the sun makes the trip to earth in about 8 minutes and 18 seconds. Traveling the same distance in your car at highway speeds would take more than 170 years.

Light changes speeds when it passes from one material to another. When light passes from air to water, it slows down to about 139,800 miles (225,000 kilometers) per second.

The color of your T-shirt on a sunny, summer day can make a big difference in how hot you feel. Darker colors absorb more light than lighter colors. To stay cooler, wear a white T-shirt on a sunny day because it reflects more light than a darker shirt.

Only 10 percent of the energy used by a regular incandescent lightbulb is changed into visible light. The rest of the energy is wasted as heat.

Telescopes use lenses or mirrors to capture the little bits of light that come to earth from stars, planets, and galaxies in space. The Hubble Space Telescope has allowed us to see galaxies more than 12 billion light-years away.

Human eyes can sense light only within the visible wavelengths on the electromagnetic spectrum. Some animals see the world in a completely different way. Rattlesnakes have sensory pits that detect infrared light. Bees see ultraviolet light.

Moonbows are rainbows that form at night. These faint rainbows form when raindrops refract light reflecting off the moon. When moonlight refracts off ice crystals in the atmosphere, bright halos called moon dogs form around the moon.

 Solar energy powers satellites and spacecraft orbiting earth. The International Space Station's huge solar panels turn sunlight into electricity, light, and heat for the astronauts living and working on the spacecraft.

MORE ABOUT

SUPER SCIENTIST

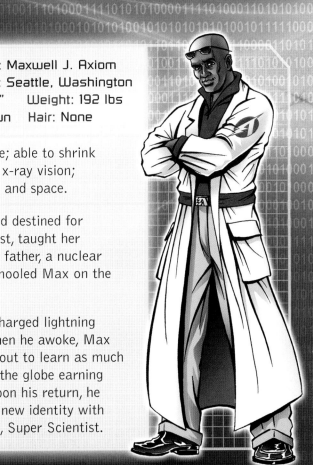

Real name: Maxwell J. Axiom
Hometown: Seattle, Washington
Height: 6' 1"   Weight: 192 lbs
Eyes: Brown   Hair: None

Super capabilities: Super intelligence; able to shrink to the size of an atom; sunglasses give x-ray vision; lab coat allows for travel through time and space.

Origin: Since birth, Max Axiom seemed destined for greatness. His mother, a marine biologist, taught her son about the mysteries of the sea. His father, a nuclear physicist and volunteer park ranger, schooled Max on the wonders of earth and sky.

One day on a wilderness hike, a megacharged lightning bolt struck Max with blinding fury. When he awoke, Max discovered a newfound energy and set out to learn as much about science as possible. He traveled the globe earning degrees in every aspect of the field. Upon his return, he was ready to share his knowledge and new identity with the world. He had become Max Axiom, Super Scientist.

GLOSSARY

atom (AT-uhm)—an element in its smallest form

concave (kahn-KAYV)—hollow and curved, like the inside of
a bowl

convex (kahn-VEKS)—curved outward, like the outside of a ball

energy (EN-ur-jee)—the ability to do work, such as moving things
or giving heat or light

fusion (FYOO-zhuhn)—the joining together of objects caused by
heating; the sun creates its energy with the process of fusion.

infrared light (IN-fruh-red LITE)—light that produces heat;
humans cannot see infrared light.

laser (LAY-zur)—a thin, intense, high-energy beam of light

opaque (oh-PAKE)—blocking light

reflection (ree-FLEK-shuhn)—the change in direction of light
bouncing off a surface

refract (ree-FRACT)—to bend light as it passes through a
substance at an angle

translucent (trans-LOO-suhnt)—letting light pass through, but not
transparent; frosted and stained glass are translucent.

transparent (transs-PAIR-uhnt)—letting light through

ultraviolet light (uhl-truh-VYE-uh-lit LITE)—an invisible form of
light that can cause sunburns

wavelength (WAYV-length)—the distances between two peaks of
a wave

READ MORE

Cooper, Christopher. *Light: From Sun to Bulbs.* Science Answers. Chicago: Heinemann, 2004.

Hamilton, Gina L. *Light: Prisms, Rainbows, and Colors.* Science at Work. Chicago: Raintree, 2004.

Juettner, Bonnie. *Light.* The Kidhaven Science Library. San Diego: Kidhaven Press, 2004.

Lilly, Melinda. *Me and My Shadow.* Read and Do Science. Vero Beach, Fla.: Rourke, 2006.

Richardson, Adele. *Light: A Question and Answer Book.* Questions and Answers: Physical Science. Mankato, Minn.: Capstone Press, 2006.

INTERNET SITES

FactHound offers a safe, fun way to find Internet sites related to this book. All of the sites on FactHound have been researched by our staff.

Here's how:
1. Visit *www.facthound.com*
2. Choose your grade level.
3. Type in this book ID **142960140X** for age-appropriate sites. You may also browse subjects by clicking on letters, or by clicking on pictures and words.
4. Click on the **Fetch It** button.

FactHound will fetch the best sites for you!